TRADITIONAL COUNTRY LIFE RECIPE SERIES

AMERICAN CHEF'S COMPANION

TRADITIONAL COUNTRY LIFE RECIPE SERIES
AMERICAN CHEF'S COMPANION
Elizabeth Brabb

Editorial Consultant, Lawrence Farms, NY
Vonnie Lawrence

Editorial Consultant, NY New York
Laurie Garvin

Book Design
Pearl Lau

Cover Illustration
Lisa Adams

Consultant
Richard J. Wall, Ph.D.

The Brick Tower Press ™
1230 Park Avenue, New York, NY 10128

Copyright © 1993 J. T. Colby & Company, Inc. New York

Brabb, Elizabeth
The Traditional Country Life Recipe Series:
American Chef's Companion — 1st Edition
Includes Index
ISBN 1-883283-01-9 softcover

Library of Congress Catalog Card
Number: 93-072648
September 1993
First Edition

INTRODUCTION

Traditional Country Life recipes appeal to the cook in all of us — recipes like grandma used to make, but with modern techniques, styles, clear step-by-step directions, and all natural ingredients. We have taken care to prepare basic, homespun, down-to-earth recipes, elegant in their simplicity and presentation, mouthwatering and delightful, uniquely American.

We have made every effort to preserve the integrity of the original recipe, some of which derive from Native Americans and early settlers of our country. In those days, the terms "medium heat," "high heat," and "low heat" all meant the same thing: put the skillet on the fire and get the chickens out of the kitchen.

For the cook who delights in the tastes of home, the **American Chef's Companion** contains over 90 recipes organized by topics including breads, soups, entrées, and desserts. We also include beverages, pickles, and preserves to provide authentic accents for the meals. The recipes chosen for this book are American folklore, researched on the farm, and presented here for the first time. If you never heard of Dixie punch, never knew how many potatoes go into potato bread, or want to make your own vanilla extract, this book is for you.

Elizabeth Brabb
New York 1993

TABLE OF CONTENTS

OLD FASHIONED
MANHATTAN CLAM CHOWDER

(1) In a skillet, add chopped salt pork and try out the fat.
(2) Add the onions and brown slightly.
(3) In a large pot add the tomatoes, carrots, celery, potatoes, browned onions, and salt pork to the water and simmer on medium heat for 1 hour. Do not boil.
(4) Add the clams and liquor, and simmer for 10 minutes.
(5) Add salt, pepper, and parsley to taste.
(6) Serve immediately.

☛INGREDIENTS:

1/2 lb. of salt pork
8 onions, diced
1 pt. of tomatoes, peeled, seeded, and chopped
3 carrots, diced
3 stalks of celery, diced
6 medium potatoes, diced
2 qts. of water
1 qt. of chowder clams, chopped; reserving the liquor
pepper, salt, and parsley to taste

SERVES 8-10

ORIGINAL NEW ENGLAND
CLAM CHOWDER

(1) Open the clams and reserve the clam liquor.

(2) Chop the clams coarsely.

(3) In a small pot, boil the potatoes for 5 to 10 minutes. Make sure they are still firm.

(4) In a large pot, melt the butter and sauté the onions until they are transparent.

(5) Add the cream, milk, and clam liquor. Heat until almost boiling, stirring constantly.

(6) Add the Worcestershire sauce and the chopped clams and simmer 3 minutes.

(7) Add the potatoes and season with salt, pepper, and dill.

(8) Serve immediately.

☞ INGREDIENTS:

1 dozen cherrystone clams
1 large potato, peeled and cubed
1/2 cup of onions, chopped
2 tbls. of butter
2 cups of heavy cream
1 qt. of milk
3 drops of Worcestershire sauce
2 tbls. of dill, chopped
salt and pepper to taste

SERVES 8

OYSTER SOUP DELUXE

(1) Open the oysters and reserve the liquor.

(2) In a saucepan, combine the liquor and the water.

(3) Season with the cayenne, nutmeg, mace, and cloves.

(4) When the mixture is almost boiling, add half the oysters and simmer for 5 minutes.

(5) Strain the soup and pour the liquid back into a saucepan with the milk.

(6) Mix egg yolks with 1 tsp. of butter and rub into a smooth paste.

(7) Rub 6 raw chopped oysters into a mixture made of the paste, salt, and a well beaten raw egg.

(8) Flour your hands and roll the "force-meat" into marble-sized balls. Set aside.

(9) Add the other half of the oysters to the soup mixture and bring almost to a boil.

(10) Add the "force-meat" balls and simmer just below a boil for three minutes or until the oysters "ruffle." Stir in 1 tbls. of butter and serve with the sliced lemon or lime.

☛ INGREDIENTS:

2 qts. of oysters, chopped fine
1 cup of water
1 tsp. of mixed nutmeg, mace, and cloves
1 pinch of cayenne pepper
2 egg yolks, hard boiled
1 tbls. plus 1 tsp. of butter
1 egg
1 qt. of milk
1 cup of flour
1 pinch of salt
sliced lemon or lime

SERVES 4

CREAM OF LEEK SOUP

(1) Cut leeks and celery into thin slices.
(2) Melt 3 tbls. of butter in a saucepan.
(3) Add leeks and celery and cook for 10 minutes, stirring constantly.
(4) In a double boiler, melt the remaining 2 tbls. of butter.
(5) Add the flour and whisk into a thick paste.
(6) Gradually add the milk, stirring after each addition until creamy.
(7) Add the potatoes and leek mixture and simmer slowly for 40 minutes.
(8) Serve immediately.

☛INGREDIENTS:

1 bunch of leeks
1 cup of celery
5 tbls. of butter
2 tbls. of flour
1 qt. of milk
2-1/2 cups of new potatoes, cooked and diced
salt and pepper to taste

SERVES 4-6

ONION SOUP

(1) Melt the butter and sauté the onions until they are golden in color.
(2) Add beef stock and simmer for 30 minutes.
(3) Add salt to taste.
(4) Serve hot with a piece of cheese toast floating on top.

Cheese Toast Cut sliced bread with a cookie cutter into shapes. Toast one side of bread shapes in the broiler. Melt 4 tbls. of butter and then add 2 tbls. of parmesan cheese. Brush the other side of each bread shape with the butter mixture and toast in broiler until golden brown.

NOTE: If using this soup in the meatloaf recipe, mince the onions.

☛INGREDIENTS:

1 large Spanish onion, thinly sliced
4 cups of beef stock
2 tbls. of butter
salt to taste
Cheese Toast (see note)

SERVES 4-6

PUMPKIN SOUP

(1) Melt the butter and sauté the onions and garlic until the onions are translucent.
(2) Add the chicken stock and bring to a boil.
(3) Add the puréed pumpkin, brown sugar, and nutmeg.
(4) Simmer for 30 minutes to blend flavors.
(5) Add the milk just before serving, heating only to warm the milk. Soup should never boil after the addition of the milk.
(6) Serve hot with Cheese Toast.

Cheese Toast Cut sliced bread with a cookie cutter. Toast one side in the broiler. Melt 4 tbls. of butter and then add 2 tbls. of parmesan cheese. Brush the other side of each bread shape with the butter mixture. Toast in broiler until golden brown.

NOTE: I like to make this soup the day before (without the milk) to blend the flavors. This soup can also be easily frozen (without the milk).

☛INGREDIENTS:

2 tbls. of butter
2 medium yellow onions
1 large clove of garlic
8 cups of chicken stock
4 cups of cooked pumpkin, puréed
1 heaping tsp. of brown sugar
1/4 tsp. of nutmeg
1 cup of milk
Cheese Toast (see note)

SERVES 8-10

OLD FASHIONED
BAKING POWDER BISCUITS

(1) Using a pastry blender or 2 forks, blend flour, baking powder, butter, and salt.
(2) In a measuring cup, beat egg and then add enough milk to equal 1 cup.
(3) Pour liquid into flour mixture all at once.
(4) Stir quickly until just blended.
(5) Drop by large tablespoon onto a greased cookie sheet (batter will be on the wet side).
(6) Bake 15-20 minutes or until lightly browned on top.

NOTE: If you want to cut biscuits with a biscuit cutter, reduce liquid to 3/4 of a cup. When mixed, place dough onto a floured pastry cloth and roll out to 1/2 inch thick. Cut with 2-inch biscuit cutter.

NOTE: To make a shortcake, add 1/4 cup of sugar to the dough.

☞ INGREDIENTS:

Preheat oven to 400° F.

2 cups of flour
4 tsp. of baking powder
5 rounded tbls. of butter
3/4 tsp. of salt
1 egg
scant cup of milk

SERVES 4

BOSTON BROWN BREAD

(1) Mix and sift together the dry
 ingredients.
(2) Add the molasses and milk.
(3) Stir until well mixed.
(4) Pour batter into a well-greased mold (no
 more than 2/3 full).
(5) Cover mold closely with foil and string
 or a tight fitting lid.
(6) Set mold on a rack in a pot filled with
 enough water so that 1/2 of the mold is
 immersed.
(7) Steam for 3-1/2 hours.
(8) Serve warm, with butter. Great with a
 baked bean supper.

NOTE: To make sour milk, add 2 tbls. of
white vinegar to 2 cups of milk. Let this
mixture sit for 15 minutes. Buttermilk is
also a good substitute.

☛ INGREDIENTS:

1 cup of rye meal
1 cup of cornmeal
1 cup of graham flour
3/4 tbls. of baking soda
1-1/2 tsp. of salt
3/4 cup of molasses
2 cups of sour milk (see note)

MAKES 1 LOAF

GINGER BREAD

(1) Cream the butter.
(2) Beat in half of the sugar.
(3) Beat egg with the rest of the sugar.
(4) Combine egg and butter mixtures.
(5) Sift dry ingredients together.
(6) Add dry ingredients to butter mixture.
(7) Add milk or hot water, and molasses.
(8) Beat until well mixed.
(9) Pour batter into a well greased bread pan.
(10) Bake for 35 minutes.

☛ INGREDIENTS:

Preheat oven to 325° F.

1/2 cup of sugar
3 tbls. of butter
1 egg
1-1/2 cups of white flour
1 tsp. of baking soda
1/8 tsp. of salt
1 tbls. of ginger
1 tsp. of cinnamon
1/2 cup of milk or hot water
1/2 cup of molasses

MAKES 1 LOAF

PEANUT BUTTER BREAD

(1) Cream the peanut butter, butter, and sugar.
(2) Beat the egg well and add to peanut butter mixture.
(3) Mix and sift together the dry ingredients.
(4) Alternately add the dry ingredients and milk to the peanut butter mixture, blending well after each addition.
(5) Beat the entire mixture well and place in a greased bread tin.
(6) Bake for 50 minutes or until a cake tester comes out clean.

☛ INGREDIENTS:
Preheat the oven to 350° F.

1 cup of peanut butter
4 tbls. of butter
1/2 cup of sugar
1 egg
3 cups of bread flour
1 tbls. plus 1 tsp. of baking powder
1/2 tsp. of salt
1 cup of milk

MAKES 3 LOAVES

SPIDER CORN BREAD

(1) Mix the dry ingredients.
(2) Beat eggs well.
(3) Add eggs and milk to dry ingredients.
(4) Melt the butter in a frying pan.
(5) Pour batter into frying pan.
(6) Cook on top of the stove for 3 minutes.
(7) Place frying pan in the oven and bake for 15-20 minutes.
(8) Serve hot with butter.

NOTE: To make sour milk, add 2 tbls. of white vinegar to 2 cups of milk. Let this mixture sit for 15 minutes before using.

NOTE: The frying pan should not have a plastic or wooden handle. A cast iron skillet is best. Before the invention of the stove the cast iron skillet was made with legs, hence the name "spider." The cook would place the spider into the hearth and put coals under and over the pan to cook the dough.

☞ INGREDIENTS:
Preheat oven to 400° F.

1 cup of cornmeal
1/2 cup of rolled oats
1 tsp. of baking soda
1 tsp. of salt
2 eggs
2 cups of sour milk (see note)
2 tbls. of butter

SERVES 4

SPOON BREAD

(1) Heat milk to nearly boiling.
(2) Gradually stir cornmeal into milk.
(3) Cook until the consistency of mush.
(4) Add the baking powder and salt.
(5) Beat the egg yolks until light.
(6) Stir a small amount of the hot mixture into the eggs.
(7) Add the egg yolk mixture to the cornmeal mixture and blend well.
(8) Beat the egg whites until stiff.
(9) Fold egg whites into cornmeal mixture.
(10) Pour into a greased soufflé dish and bake for 30 minutes.
(11) Serve at once with plenty of butter.

NOTE: You can serve this recipe as is for dinner, or sprinkle confectioners' sugar on top just before serving for breakfast.

☞ INGREDIENTS:
   Preheat oven to 350° F.

1 pt. of milk
1/2 cup of cornmeal
1/2 tsp. of baking powder
1 tsp. of salt
3 eggs, separated

SERVES 4

WHITE BREAD

(1) Work yeast and sugar together with the back of a spoon in a small bowl until the yeast liquefies.

(2) Add 2-2/3 cups of the lukewarm liquid and one tbls. of flour. Set aside to rise.

(3) Sift the remaining flour and salt together into a large mixing bowl, making a hollow in the center.

(4) Melt butter in remaining lukewarm liquid.

(5) Pour this liquid and the yeast mixture into the hollow.

(6) Gradually work in the flour.

(7) Knead until dough is smooth and elastic.

(8) Turn dough in a lightly greased bowl, so that all sides are greased. This will prevent a skin from forming, cover with a damp cloth and set aside in a warm draftless corner until dough has doubled in bulk (approximately 3 to 4 hours).

(9) Turn dough onto a floured board and divide into loaves.

(10) Knead each loaf for less than a minute.

☛ INGREDIENTS:
Preheat oven to 375° F.

1 cake of compressed yeast
2 tsp. of sugar
1 qt. of lukewarm liquid (milk, water, or combination of the two)
12 cups of bread flour
3 tsp. of salt
2 tbls. of butter, melted

MAKES 3 LOAVES

(11) Place dough in greased bread pans, cover and let rise until bulk is doubled (approximately 1 hour).

(12) Brush each loaf with melted butter.

(13) Bake for 40 - 60 minutes according to the size of the loaves.

FRENCH BREAD

(1) Sift the flour into a large mixing bowl leaving a hollow in the center.
(2) In a separate bowl, work the yeast and sugar together with the back of a spoon.
(3) Add the water and salt to the yeast mixture and mix. Then pour this mixture into the hollow of the sifted flour.
(4) Work into an elastic dough, cover with a damp cloth and set aside in a warm, draftless corner for approximately 4 hours. The dough will double in bulk.
(5) Knead the dough gently for under a minute. Cover again and let rise to double its bulk.
(6) Divide into 3 or 4 portions and stretch into long, cylindrical loaves.
(7) Lay loaves on floured baking sheets. Cover again and let rise to double their bulk.
(8) Bake for 1 hour and 10 minutes.
(9) Brush each loaf with a cornstarch glaze and bake an additional 10 minutes.

☛ INGREDIENTS:
Preheat oven to 400° F.

12 cups of bread flour
1 cake of compressed yeast
2 tsp. of sugar
1 qt. of lukewarm water
2 tsp. of salt

MAKES 3-4 LOAVES

Cornstarch Glaze
1/2 tsp. of cornstarch
2 tsp. of cold water
1/3 cup of boiling water

(1) Moisten the cornstarch with the cold water.
(2) Pour the boiling water over it, and cook for 5 minutes.
NOTE: French bread is always made with water, not milk, and must be thoroughly baked.

POTATO BREAD

(1) Work yeast into the water to dissolve.

(2) Boil potatoes in 4 cups of water until soft enough to mash without lumps.

(3) Remove pan from flame and cool.

(4) When cool add the milk and yeast.

(5) In a large bowl, sift flour, sugars, and salt.

(6) Slowly add potato mixture, mixing after each addition.

(7) If dough is sticky, add more flour to make dough soft and smooth.

(8) Knead for 1 minute and place in a lightly greased bowl.

(9) Cover with a damp towel, place in a warm draftless corner and let rise until double in bulk.

(10) Punch down and knead for 7 minutes.

(11) Let rise again in the greased bowl until double in bulk.

(12) Punch down again and knead for 1 minute.

(13) Divide into 3 loaves and place in greased pans.

(14) Cover and let rise again.

(15) Brush tops with melted butter.

(16) Bake for 50 minutes

☞ INGREDIENTS:

Preheat oven to 350° F.

2-1/2 cakes of compressed yeast
1/2 cup of lukewarm water
2 medium potatoes, peeled
4 cups of water
1 cup of milk
10 cups of flour, sifted
1/4 cup of sugar
1 tbls. of brown sugar
2 tbls. of salt
2 tbls. of butter, melted

MAKES 3 LOAVES

RAISIN BREAD

(1) Scald the milk and cool it until lukewarm.
(2) Crumble the yeast cake into milk.
(3) Add 2 cups of flour and beat thoroughly.
(4) Set this mixture aside until light and frothy.
(5) Cream the butter and sugar until the mixture is light.
(6) Add the raisins and salt and mix well.
(7) Combine the remaining flour with the raisin mixture.
(8) Add this mixture to the yeast mixture.
(9) Knead dough on a floured pastry board thoroughly, approximately 5 minutes, cover with a damp cloth and set aside in a warm, draftless corner for approximately 3 hours. The dough will double in bulk.
(10) Divide into two portions; knead each portion for 1 minute to break up gaseous bubbles; place in two greased bread pans.
(11) Cover again and let rise to double their bulk.
(12) Bake for 40 minutes.

☛ INGREDIENTS:
Preheat oven to 350° F.

1-1/2 cups of milk
1 cake of compressed yeast
6-1/2 cups of bread flour
3 tbls. of butter
1/2 cup of sugar
1 cup of raisins
2/3 tsp. of salt
Bread flour to knead

2 LOAVES

16

EASY CHEESE SOUFFLÉ

(1) Alternately, layer bread and cheese in a soufflé dish.
(2) Beat eggs with milk.
(3) Add salt, thyme, Tabasco sauce, and mustard.
(4) Pour egg mixture over bread and cheese.
(5) Bake for 2 hours.
(6) Serve immediately upon removing from oven. As the soufflé cools, it falls.

☞ INGREDIENTS:

Preheat oven to 250° F.

6 slices of white bread, cut in half
2 cups of grated sharp cheddar cheese
3 eggs
2 cups of milk
1 tsp. of salt
1/2 tsp. of thyme
1/2 tsp. of Tabasco sauce
1/2 tsp. of dry mustard

SERVES 4

WELSH RABBIT

(1) Lightly beat egg yolks with stale beer; set aside.

(2) In a double boiler melt the butter and cheese, stirring constantly.

(3) While stirring, add the mustard, salt, cayenne, and Worcestershire sauce.

(4) Add egg and beer mixture.

(5) Keep stirring until sauce has a creamy thickness, then a bit more for real smoothness.

(6) Poor over toast points and serve immediately.

NOTE: Tomatoes are also a good addition to this recipe. Lay the tomatoes on the toast points and then cover with the cheese sauce.

☛ INGREDIENTS:

2 egg yolks
1/2 cup of stale beer
2 tbls. of butter
3 cups of grated
   cheddar cheese
1/2 tsp. dry mustard
1/2 tsp. of salt
dash of cayenne
1 tsp. of Worcestershire sauce
8 slices of toast

SERVES 4

MEATLOAF

(1) Mix all of the ingredients, except the bacon.
(2) Shape into long oblong shape.
(3) Lay bacon across the top.
(4) Bake for one hour.
(5) Remove from oven and let sit 10 minutes.
(6) Serve immediately.

NOTE: Leftovers make terrific meatloaf sandwiches.

☛ INGREDIENTS:
Preheat oven to 350° F.

2-2/3 cups of onion soup
2 lbs. of ground beef
1 cup of bread crumbs
2 eggs, beaten
5 slices of bacon
SERVES 8

POT ROAST

(1) In a large kettle, heat oil.
(2) Add the onions and garlic, sauté until lightly browned.
(3) Add the meat and brown on all sides.
(4) Add the beef stock.
(5) Cover the kettle and simmer for 3 hours.
(6) Add the sliced carrots and mushrooms and cook for another 1/2 hour.
(7) Serve with egg noodles.

☛ INGREDIENTS:

3 tbls. of oil
1 large onion, sliced
1 clove of garlic, minced
1-1/2 lb. chuck roast
2 cups of beef stock
6 carrots, sliced
1/2 lb. of mushrooms, sliced
egg noodles

SERVES 6

PLANKED STEAK

(1) Char the plank on the coals of the grill or the rack in the oven to heat thoroughly.
(2) Brush meat with oil and season with garlic.
(3) Broil or barbecue meat for 6 minutes *(3 minutes on each side)*.
(4) Place meat on the plank.
(5) Bake for 10 minutes in your oven or on the grill, 5 - 6 inches from coals.
(6) Serve immediately.

NOTE: Make mashed potatoes ahead and place them on the plank around the meat. They will become golden brown on top. Mushrooms or onions or both are also a delicious addition.

TO CLEAN THE PLANK: Rub the plank gently first with sandpaper, then with salt. Store in a cool airy place until next use.

NOTE: Native Americans taught early settlers how to cook meat outdoors using this method.

☛ INGREDIENTS:
Preheat the oven to 350° F., or prepare the barbecue

1 plank of hickory, oak, cherry, etc. 2 inches thick and larger than the steak
2 lbs. of London Broil, 1-1/2 to 2 inches thick
3 tbls. of oil
1 garlic clove, minced

SERVES 6-8

SCALLOPED
CORNED BEEF AND CABBAGE

(1) Melt butter and sauté onions until softened.

(2) Whisk in flour until the mixture is smooth.

(3) Whisk in milk, pepper, mustard, and caraway seeds.

(4) Cook until the sauce almost comes to a boil, whisking often.

(5) Stir in corned beef and cabbage; combine well.

(6) Grease a 1-1/2 quart glass or ceramic baking dish.

(7) Add corned beef mixture and bake for 15 minutes; sprinkle the cheese on top and bake another 10 minutes or until bubbling and lightly browned on top.

☛ INGREDIENTS:
Preheat oven to 350° F.

8 tbls. of butter
1 medium onion, thinly sliced
1/4 cup of flour
2-1/2 cups of milk
Freshly ground pepper to taste
4 tbls. of mustard
1 tsp. of caraway seeds
2 cups of diced cooked corned beef
6 cups of thinly shredded leftover cooked cabbage
1/2 tsp. of oil
1/2 cup of grated cheddar cheese

SERVES 6

SHEPHERD'S PIE

(1) In a saucepan, brown meat with the garlic, onion, and rosemary.
(2) Set the meat aside in a bowl.
(3) Melt the butter in the used sauce pan.
(4) Gradually whisk in the flour.
(5) Add the beef broth.
(6) Cook this mixture until the gravy has thickened.
(7) Add the meat, salt, pepper, and peas.
(8) Place this mixture in a large pie plate.
(9) Top with the mashed potatoes.
(10) Bake for 35-45 minutes.

☛ INGREDIENTS:
Preheat oven to 375° F.

1-1/2 lbs. of hamburger
1 large clove of garlic
1 small onion
1/2 tsp. of rosemary
4 tbls. of butter
2 tbls. of flour
3/4 cup of beef broth
　salt and pepper to taste
1-1/2 cups of peas
4 medium potatoes, boiled and mashed without milk

SERVES 6

BAKED
APPLE CIDER CHICKEN

(1) Place cinnamon, cloves, and allspice in a bag made of cheesecloth.
(2) In a saucepan, simmer the apple cider with the spice bag, onion, and garlic.
(3) Dip each chicken breast in the butter and dredge in the bread crumbs.
(4) In a lightly oiled baking dish arrange the chicken.
(5) Bake for 45 minutes.
(6) Remove the spice bag; add the apple cider mixture to the chicken and bake for another 15 minutes.
(7) Serve immediately.

☞ INGREDIENTS:
Preheat oven to 350° F.

2 cups of apple cider
1 cinnamon stick, broken
4 whole cloves
4 whole allspice
1 small onion, thinly sliced
1 clove of garlic, finely chopped
4 chicken breasts, split, skinned, and boned
6 tbls. of melted butter
1-1/2 cups of bread crumbs

SERVES 6

BAKED
HONEY LEMON CHICKEN

(1) Mix honey, butter, and lemon vinegar.
(2) Brush underside of each chicken breast with this mixture.
(3) Bake for 30 minutes, skin side down.
(4) Brush top of each breast with lemon mixture.
(5) Bake for 30 minutes, skin side up.
(6) If needed, broil until the skin is golden brown.
(7) Serve immediately.

☛ INGREDIENTS:

Preheat oven to 350° F.

6 tbls. of honey, warm
1 tbls. of butter, melted
3 tbls. of lemon vinegar
4 chicken breasts, split

SERVES 6

LEMON CHICKEN

(1) Pound chicken breasts until flat.
(2) Brown chicken breasts in 1 tbls. each of butter and oil.
(3) Remove chicken from pan.
(4) Add the chicken stock, remaining butter, and lemon juice to the pan and bring to a simmer.
(5) Return chicken to the pan and cover and simmer for approximately 15 minutes over a medium flame, basting often.
(6) Sprinkle with parsley and serve with rice.

☛INGREDIENTS:

4 chicken breasts, split, boned,   and skinned
5 tbls. of butter
1 tbls. of oil
3/4 cup of chicken stock
2 tbls. of freshly squeezed lemon juice
2 tbls. of parsley

SERVES 6-8

PRESSED CHICKEN

(1) Boil chicken and garlic in enough water to cover, until meat falls off bones.
(2) Discard the skin and remove the meat from the bones.
(3) Finely chop chicken and onion.
(4) Mix in the salt and pepper and put into a casserole dish.
(5) Simmer bones in the chicken broth for another hour.
(6) Remove bones and fat from broth.
(7) Simmer broth until reduced to 4 cups.
(8) Cool broth and then add gelatin.
(9) Pour over chicken and chill until firm.
(10) Serve on lettuce and garnish with mayonnaise or serve as an appetizer on crackers.

NOTE: This recipe may also be seasoned with curry, dill, or basil. Leftovers can be frozen.

☛INGREDIENTS:

7 lb. roasting chicken
water
2 cloves of garlic
1 large onion
salt and pepper to taste
2 tbls. of unflavored gelatin

SERVES 12

26

BAKED APPLES STUFFED WITH SAUSAGES

(1) Scoop out the centers of the apples, leaving a thick shell.
(2) Cut all the pulp possible from the core.
(3) Chop up pulp and mix with the meat.
(4) Refill the apples with this mixture, until heaping and place in baking dish.
(5) Add water to baking dish.
(6) Bake in the oven, basting frequently for approximately 35 minutes.
(7) Serve with maple syrup.

☛INGREDIENTS:
Preheat oven to 350° F.

6 good-sized tart apples
1 cup of sausage meat
1 cup of water

SERVES 6

HOMEMADE SAUSAGE

(1) Grind pork and fat twice (or have your butcher grind it).
(2) Season with salt, pepper, and sage.
(3) Form into patties.
(4) Freeze until needed.
(5) Cook in a skillet, or add to other recipes.

☛INGREDIENTS:
3 lbs. of pork
1 lb. of fresh pork fat
3 tsp. of salt
1-1/2 tsp. of pepper
1-1/2 tsp. of dried sage, rubbed to a powder

SERVES 12

CROWN ROAST OF PORK

(1) Each rib should be trimmed as lamb chops are cut when frenched, but do not separate the ribs. The sections of meat are then turned so that the bones are on the outside, and fastened together in a circle with skewers and string. This may be done by your butcher.

(2) Soak the bread crumbs in cold water and squeeze dry. Mix with the walnut meats and spices.

(3) Place the stuffing in the center of the roast and cover the tips of the bones with foil.

(4) Put the meat in the oven and cook for 30 minutes.

(5) Add a cup of water to pan and lower the heat to 350 ° F. and continue roasting for 1 hour, basting frequently.

(6) Sprinkle the roast with salt and pepper 1/2 hour before done.

(7) Parboil the onions in slightly salted water and place an onion on the end of each rib in place of the foil 10 minutes before the roast is done. Baste with drippings.

(8) Make a gravy out of the drippings, flour, and boiling water.

☛INGREDIENTS:

Preheat oven to 500° F.

12 ribs of pork -
  2 racks of 6 ribs each
2 cups of dry bread crumbs
1/4 cup of walnut meats, chopped
1-1/2 tsp. of salt
1/4 tsp. of pepper
1/2 tsp. of summer savory
12 small white onions
4 tbls. of flour
2 tbls. of chopped tart pickles
1/4 tsp. of paprika

SERVES 8-12

(9) Add the pickle and stir to blend.
(10) Add the salt, pepper, and paprika to taste.

DILLED PORK CHOPS WITH ZUCCHINI

(1) Mix together flour, dill, salt and pepper, 1-1/2 tbls. of parmesan cheese.
(2) Dredge pork chops in this mixture.
(3) Brown pork chops in a mixture of oil and butter.
(4) Add water and cover pork chops with onions.
(5) Cover and simmer over a low flame for 15 minutes.
(6) Cover pork chops with zucchini.
(7) Mix together leftover flour mixture with paprika, and remaining parmesan cheese.
(8) Sprinkle this flour mixture on top of the zucchini.
(9) Cover and cook for 30 minutes, basting 3 times. (Add water if needed.)

☛INGREDIENTS:

3 tbls. of flour
1 tbls. dill
1-1/2 tsp. of salt and pepper, blended
4-1/2 tbls. of grated parmesan cheese
6 large pork chops
1 tbls. of butter
1 tbls. of oil
1/3 cup of water
1 small onion, sliced
6 small zucchini, sliced
1/2 tsp. of paprika

SERVES 4-6

SCALLOPED
HAM AND POTATOES

(1) Melt the butter and sauté onions
until softened.
(2) Gradually add the flour, whisking
after each addition. Cook until mixture
begins to bubble.
(3) Add the milk, a little at a time,
whisking constantly until thickened.
(4) Add salt and pepper.
(5) Add the potatoes.
(6) Soak the bread crumbs in water
and squeeze until dry.
(7) Put into a buttered baking dish in layers:
bread, ham, creamed potatoes, bread,
ham, etc. End with bread crumbs.
(8) Brown in the oven.

☛INGREDIENTS:
Preheat oven to 500° F.

2 tbls. of butter
1 small onion
2 tbls. of flour
1 cup of cold milk
1/2 tsp. of salt
1/4 tsp. of pepper
1 cup of cooked,
diced potatoes
2 cups of stale bread crumbs
1 cup of cooked, minced ham

SERVES 4-6

BAKED FISH

(1) Marinate the fish in the wine for 2 hours.
(2) Drain fish.
(3) Coat fish with the bread crumbs.
(4) Mix together the mayonnaise, sour cream, and minced onion.
(5) Spread mayonnaise mixture over fish.
(6) Place fish in a baking dish.
(7) Sprinkle the fish with more bread crumbs and paprika.
(8) Bake for approximately 14 minutes or until fish is flaky.

☛INGREDIENTS:
Preheat oven to 425° F.

2 lbs. of flounder, perch, or haddock
1 cup of dry white wine
1 cup of fine dry bread crumbs
1 cup of mayonnaise
1 cup of sour cream
1/2 cup of onion, minced

SERVES 6

PLANKED SALMON

(1) Char the plank to heat thoroughly.
(2) Brush the charred side of the plank with oil or butter, then with 1/2 a lemon.
(3) Place the fish, skin side down, on the plank.
(4) Top with onion and remaining lemon, sliced.
(5) Position the plank 5 to 6 inches above coals or heating element.
(6) Cook the salmon approximately 10 minutes for each inch of thickness.
(7) Garnish with sprigs of dill.

NOTE: Small baked potatoes and vegetables may be placed around the fish while cooking to give them special flavor. Serve as is, on the plank. Cod, haddock, or halibut may also be planked but require frequent basting. Richer fish such as bluefish, shad, and mackerel will require less basting.

TO CLEAN THE PLANK: Rub the plank gently first with sandpaper then with salt. Store in a cool, airy place until next use.

☛INGREDIENTS:
   Preheat oven to 350° F., or prepare the barbecue

1 plank of hickory, oak, cherry, etc. 2-inches thick and larger than the fish
2 tbls. of butter or olive oil
1-1/2 lemons
2 lbs. of salmon
1 small onion, thinly sliced
4 sprigs of dill, for garnish

SERVES 4

Note: Native Americans taught early settlers how to cook fish outdoors using this method.

BAKED LOBSTER
WITH CREAM SAUCE

(1) In a large pot, put the lobsters into boiling water. When the water boils again, cook for 2 minutes and drain.

(2) Place the lobsters in a large baking pan, shell side up, and bake for 12 minutes.

(3) Break off the claws, and crack them in several places to expose the meat.

(4) Split the remaining body of the lobster in half lengthwise.

(5) With a spoon remove the insides of the lobster from the head down to the beginning of the tail section and place into a saucepan.

(6) Add the shallots, salt, and pepper, and bring to a boil, stirring constantly.

(7) Reduce the heat to a simmer, add the lemon juice and cook for about 2 minutes.

(8) Pour the mixture into a colander lined with cheesecloth.

(9) Return sauce to the saucepan and bring to a simmer. Add the cream, butter, and tarragon.

☛ INGREDIENTS:

Preheat oven to 500° F.

4 (1 to 1-1/2 lb.) lobsters
8 cups of water
2 tbls. shallots, chopped
salt and pepper to taste
2 tbls. of lemon juice
1/2 cup heavy cream
3 tbls. butter
1 tsp. fresh tarragon, chopped

SERVES 4

(10) Place the lobster halves and claws shell side down on a serving dish.

(11) Pour the sauce over the lobsters and serve.

CLAM PIE

(1) Mix the clams and onions.
(2) In a bowl, add the milk and clam
    liquor to the bread .
(3) Add the clam mixture
    and the seasonings.
(4) Place this mixture in a large pie plate.
(5) Place the tomato slices on top and
    sprinkle the cheese on top to cover.
(6) Bake for 30 minutes or until the
    cheese is bubbling.

☛INGREDIENTS:
    Preheat oven to 350° F.

18 chowder clams, minced;
    reserve 1/2 cup of liquor
1 medium onion, minced
8 slices of bread, crumbled
1/2 cup of milk
1/2 tsp. of salt
1/8 tsp. of pepper
2 tomatoes, sliced
2 cups of grated sharp
    cheddar cheese

SERVES 4

ASPARAGUS WITH CREAMY LEMON VINAIGRETTE

(1) Whisk mayonnaise with oil until smooth.
(2) Add the vinegar and whisk.
(3) Snap off pale ends of the asparagus and discard. Peel botrtom portion with a vegetable peeler.
(4) Steam asparagus until tender.
(5) Remove asparagus from steamer and spoon on vinaigrette.
(6) Serve warm or cool.

☞INGREDIENTS:

1-1/2 tbls. of oil
1-1/2 tbls. of mayonnaise
1/2 cup of lemon vinegar
2 lbs. of asparagus

SERVES 4

LEMON CARROTS

(1) Julienne carrots and cut into 4-inch pieces.
(2) Blanch carrots in enough water to cover.
(3) In a saucepan, melt butter.
(4) Add sugar, paprika, and lemon juice.
(5) Bring to a simmer.
(6) Add carrots and simmer for 10 minutes, tossing frequently.
(7) Serve immediately.

NOTE: You can extract more juice out of a warm lemon.

☞INGREDIENTS:

8-10 carrots, peeled
3 tbls. of butter
2 tbls. of sugar
1/2 tsp. of paprika
juice of 1/2 lemon

SERVES 6

CORN PUDDING

(1) Remove kernels of corn from cobs
with a knife.
(2) Process kernels in a food processor.
(3) In a bowl blend the flour and butter together.
(4) Add the corn, eggs, milk,
and sugar, to the mixture.
(5) Pour into a greased baking dish.
(6) Place baking dish in the pan of water.
(7) Bake for 45 minutes.

NOTE: This recipe was influenced by Native
American cookery. Europeans used refined
cornmeal instead of fresh corn.

☛INGREDIENTS:
Preheat oven to 325° F. and
place a pan of water in
the oven

6 large ears of corn
1 tbls. of flour
1 tbls. of butter, melted
3 eggs
1 cup of milk
1 tsp. of sugar
1 pinch of salt

SERVES 4

FRIED TOMATOES

(1) Remove ends from the tomatoes
   then cut tomatoes in half.
(2) Season with salt and pepper.
(3) Coat with bread crumbs.
(4) Place butter in pan and heat
   until hot enough to brown.
(5) Add tomatoes and brown on both sides.
(6) Lower heat and cook slowly for 10 minutes.
(7) Add cream and bring to a simmer.
(8) Serve immediately.

☛INGREDIENTS:

4 tomatoes, half ripe
salt and pepper to taste
1 cup of bread crumbs
2 tbls. of butter
1-1/2 cups of cream

SERVES 4

ROASTED WINTER VEGETABLES

(1) Place cut vegetables in a large enough baking dish to accommodate one layer of vegetables.
(2) Sprinkle rosemary on top of vegetables.
(3) Drizzle olive oil on top and mix to coat all the vegetables with oil.
(4) Pour chicken stock over vegetables.
(5) Bake for approximately 1 hour. Toss the vegetables occasionally to prevent burning.

☞INGREDIENTS:

Preheat oven to 350° F.

8 carrots, peeled and cut into
   1-inch pieces
1 bunch of celery, cut into
   1-inch pieces
12 small red bliss potatoes,
   cut into quarters
24 small white onions
2 tbls. of rosemary
1/2 cup of olive oil
1/2 cup of chicken stock

SERVES 8

SAVOY CABBAGE

(1) Steam quartered cabbage in 2-3 inches of water until slightly tender. Reserve broth.
(2) Melt butter and sauté onions and garlic until onions are transparent.
(3) Add flour to the onion mixture. Whisk into a paste.
(4) Add cabbage broth and cook until thickened, stirring constantly.
(5) Shred cabbage and add to the sauce.
(6) Season with salt, pepper, and nutmeg.
(7) Simmer over a low flame for 10 minutes.
(8) Serve immediately.

☛INGREDIENTS:

1 whole Savoy cabbage, quartered
1/4 lb. of unsalted butter
5 medium onions, diced
1-2 cloves of garlic, minced
1/4 cup of flour
salt, pepper, and nutmeg to taste

SERVES 6

MERINGUES

(1) Beat egg whites until they form soft peaks.
(2) Gradually add the sugar, a spoonful at a time, beating well after each addition.
(3) Add vanilla and beat until stiff peaks form.
(4) Shape the meringues by dropping from a spoon onto the cookie sheet covered with brown paper or parchment.
(5) Turn off the oven and place cookies in oven.
(6) Leave cookies in the oven for at least 6 hours or preferably overnight.

NOTE: Be sure not to open the oven until the cookies are done.

☛INGREDIENTS:
   Preheat oven to 350° F.

3 cups of egg whites, at room temperature
1 cup of confectioners' sugar, sifted
1 tsp. of vanilla extract
brown paper or parchment

OATMEAL COOKIES

(1) Rub butter into sugar.
(2) Add egg and mix well.
(3) Mix rolled oats, salt, and baking powder.
(4) Add to butter mixture.
(5) Drop by teaspoons onto a
greased cookie sheet.
(6) Bake for 5-7 minutes, or until lightly
browned on top.

☛INGREDIENTS:
Preheat oven to 375° F.

1 tbls. of butter
1/2 cup of sugar
1 egg, beaten
1-1/2 cups of rolled oats
1/4 tsp. of salt
1/2 tsp. of baking powder

MAKES APPROX.
20 COOKIES

PEANUT BUTTER COOKIES

(1) Mix peanut butter, sugar, and eggs.
   Be sure to mix well.
(2) Roll the dough into 3/4-inch balls.
(3) Bake for 10-12 minutes.
(4) Remove from the oven and cool.

Peanut Butter Cookies
with Hershey's Kisses
Needs 9 oz. of Hershey's
Chocolate Kisses

When cookie is cool, press chocolate kiss into the center of each cookie. Cookie should be cool enough so that the kiss will not melt but warm enough to be able to push the kiss into the cookie.

☛INGREDIENTS:
   Preheat oven to 350° F.

18 oz. of smooth peanut butter
1-1/2 cups of sugar
2 eggs

MAKES APPROX.
80 COOKIES

CHOCOLATE POTATO CAKE

(1) Cream butter and sugar.

(2) Beat egg yolks and add to butter mixture.

(3) Sift flour and baking powder together.

(4) Add chocolate, mashed potatoes, milk and vanilla to creamed butter.

(5) Add the flour mixture and blend well.

(6) Beat egg whites until stiff, but not dry.

(7) Carefully fold egg whites into batter.

(8) Pour batter into greased and floured 8-inch layer cake pans.

(9) Bake for 15-20 minutes.

NOTE: Frost with a fluffy butter cream frosting.

☛INGREDIENTS:

Preheat oven to 375° F.

2/3 cup of butter
2 cups of sugar
4 eggs, separated
2-1/2 cups of flour
2 tsp. of baking powder
1/2 cup of grated chocolate, firmly packed
1 cup of mashed potatoes, with milk and butter
3/4 cup of milk
2 tsp. of vanilla extract

SERVES 8

MYSTERY MOCHA CAKE

(1) Mix and sift 3/4 cup of granulated sugar, flour, baking powder, and salt.
(2) Melt chocolate and butter in a double boiler.
(3) Add chocolate mixture to sifted flour and blend well.
(4) Combine the milk and vanilla.
(5) Add to chocolate mixture and blend well.
(6) Pour dough into an 8 x 5 x 3-inch loaf pan.
(7) Combine remaining granulated sugar, brown sugar, and unsweetened cocoa.
(8) Sprinkle this mixture over the dough.
(9) Pour strong cold coffee over the top.
(10) Bake for 40 minutes.
(11) Cool and then chill before unmolding.
(12) Serve with whipped cream or ice cream.

☛INGREDIENTS:
Preheat oven to 350° F.

1-1/4 cups of granulated sugar
1 cup of flour
2 tsp. of baking powder
1/8 tsp. of salt
1 oz. of bitter chocolate
2 tbls. of butter
1/2 cup of milk
1 tsp. of vanilla
1/2 cup of brown sugar
4 tbls. of unsweetened cocoa
1 cup of strong cold coffee

SERVES 6

SUNSHINE CAKE

(1) Cream the butter and sugar together.
(2) Beat eggs until very light.
(3) Add eggs to creamed butter.
(4) Sift the flour with the baking
    powder and salt.
(5) Mix flour mixture with the squash.
(6) Combine both mixtures
    and mix thoroughly.
(7) Combine hot milk and lemon extract.
(8) Add to squash mixture.
(9) Bake in greased and floured 8-inch
    layer cake pans for 20-25 minutes.
(10) Frost with lemon frosting.

☛INGREDIENTS:
   Preheat oven to 375° F.

1/4 cup of butter
1 cup of sugar
2 eggs
1-1/2 cups of pastry flour
2 tsp. of baking powder
1/2 tsp. of salt
1/2 cup of cooked,
   puréed butternut squash
1/2 cup of hot milk
1 tsp. of lemon extract

SERVES 8

WHITE CAKE

(1) Cream the butter and sugar together.
(2) Beat the egg yolks well and add to creamed butter and sugar.
(3) Sift together the dry ingredients.
(4) Add dry ingredients and milk alternately to the creamed butter and sugar, beating well after each addition.
(5) Add the extracts.
(6) Beat the egg whites until they form stiff peaks, but are not dry.
(7) Carefully fold in the egg whites.
(8) Grease and flour 8-inch layer cake pans.
(9) Add batter and bake for 30 minutes.
(10) Frost with the Chocolate Butter Cream Frosting on the next page.

☛INGREDIENTS:
Preheat oven to 375° F.

1/2 cup of butter
1 cup of sugar
2 eggs, separated
1-1/2 cups of pastry flour
2-1/2 tsp. of baking powder
1/4 tsp. of salt
1/2 cup of milk
1/4 tsp. of orange extract
1/4 tsp. of vanilla extract

SERVES 8

BUTTER CREAM FROSTING

(1) Cream butter and gradually add 1/4 cup of confectioners' sugar.
(2) Stir in unbeaten egg yolk.
(3) Add vanilla.
(4) Alternately add the cream and remaining confectioners' sugar.
(5) Frost the cake.

CHOCOLATE BUTTER CREAM FROSTING
Add 1-1/2 squares of unsweetened melted chocolate after first 1/4 cup of sugar has been added.

MOCHA FROSTING
Add 1 tbls. of cocoa to sugar. Use strong coffee instead of cream.

LEMON FROSTING
Substitute lemon juice for the cream and 1 tsp. of lemon zest for the vanilla.

ORANGE FROSTING
Substitute orange juice for the cream and 1 tsp. of orange zest for the vanilla.

☞INGREDIENTS:

4 tbls. of butter
2 cups of confectioners' sugar
1 egg yolk
1 tsp. of vanilla
2 tbls. of whipping cream

COVERS 1 CAKE

PEACH CRUNCH

TO MAKE FRUIT FILLING:
(1) Mix together the peaches, flour, and 1 cup of sugar.
(2) Put into a 9 x 13-inch baking dish.
(3) Combine the other cup of sugar, water, cornstarch, and vanilla.
(4) Cook this mixture over a medium flame until thick and clear.
(5) Pour over peach mixture.

TO MAKE TOPPING:
(1) Mix together the flour, brown sugar, rolled oats, and butter.
(2) Crumble topping over peaches mixture. Bake for 45 minutes.

NOTE: Strawberries or blueberries can be substituted for the peaches for a delicious dessert.

INGREDIENTS:
Preheat oven to 350° F.

Fruit Filling:
6 cups of peaches, diced
6 tbls. of flour
2 cups of sugar
1 cup of water
2 rounded tbls. of cornstarch
1 tbls. of vanilla

TOPPING:
1-1/2 cups of flour
1 cup of brown sugar, firmly packed
1-1/4 cups of rolled oats
1 cup of butter, melted

SERVES 10

PIE CRUST

(1) Blend flour, salt, and butter with a fork or pastry blender until little "peas" form.
(2) Add water, a little at a time, until dough sticks together.
(3) Roll out dough into a log shape with hands.
(4) Fold log in half and cut at crease.
(5) Form each half of log into a round ball.
(6) With a floured rolling pin on a floured surface roll the dough out large enough to accommodate the pie plate.

NOTE: The extra dough can be frozen.

☛INGREDIENTS:

2 cups of flour
1/2 tsp. of salt
2/3 cup of butter
3 tbls. of water

MAKES 2 PIE SHELLS

STRAWBERRY PIE

(1) Mix cornstarch with some of the strawberry juice from the crushed berries, stir until well mixed.
(2) Mix crushed berries, cornstarch mixture, and sugar.
(3) Bring to a boil and simmer one minute. .
(4) Cool to lukewarm.
(5) Fill crust 1/2 full with raw berries.
(6) Cover with 1/2 of glaze.
(7) Add more berries and top with remainder of glaze .
(8) Decorate with whole berries.
(9) Chill.
(10) Serve with whipped cream.

NOTE: Prepare 5 to 6 hours before serving.

☛INGREDIENTS:

3 rounded tbls. of cornstarch
1-1/2 cups of
    crushed strawberries
3/4 cup of sugar
1-1/2 cups of
    halved strawberries
1 8-inch baked pie shell

SERVES 8

LEMON MERINGUE PIE

(1) Mix together 1 cup of sugar, cornstarch, and salt.

(2) Add boiling water and stir over flame.

(3) Cook until thick.

(4) Beat egg yolks.

(5) Mix egg yolks, lemon juice and zest.

(6) Add this to sugar mixture .

(7) Pour this mixture into the baked pie shell.

(8) Beat egg whites with remaining 3 tbls. of sugar, adding 1 tbls. at a time.

(9) Beat egg whites until they form soft peaks, but are not dry.

(10) Spoon onto lemon mixture.

(11) Place in the oven and bake for 10 minutes or until the meringue is lightly browned.

(12) Cool in refrigerator before serving.

☛INGREDIENTS:

Preheat oven to 375° F.

1 cup plus 3 tbls. of sugar
3 heaping tbls. of cornstarch
1 pinch of salt
2-1/2 cups of boiling water
3 eggs, separated
juice and zest of 3 small lemons
1 baked pie shell

SERVES 8

BAKED LEMON PUDDING

(1) Cream the butter and the sugar together.
(2) Beat the egg yolks to a froth and add to creamed butter.
(3) Add grated lemon zest and strained juice of the lemons. Mix well.
(4) Line a shallow tart dish with puff pastry and add lemon mixture.
(5) Bake for 40 minutes .

NOTE: Our research suggests this recipe was a harbinger of Lemon Meringue Pie.

INGREDIENTS:
   Preheat oven to 350° F.

4 egg yolks
1/2 cup of sugar
juice and grated zest of
   1-1/2 lemons
1/2 cup of butter, warmed
puff pastry recipe

SERVES 6

OLD FASHIONED
RICE PUDDING

(1) Mix together the milk, rice, sugar, and salt.
(2) Pour into a baking dish and bake for
     15-20 minutes.
(3) Remove from oven and reduce
     oven heat to 325° F.
(4) Skim off the crust which has
     formed during baking.
(5) Sprinkle with nutmeg.
(6) Bake at 325° F. for 2 hours.
(7) Serve plain or with whipped cream.

☛INGREDIENTS:
   Preheat oven to 450° F.

1 qt. of milk
3 tbls. of rice, uncooked
4 tbls. of sugar
1 pinch of salt
nutmeg for top (optional)

SERVES 8

RHUBARB TAPIOCA DESSERT

(1) Combine all of the ingredients and cook for 15 minutes.
(2) Chill in small glass dessert dishes or one large dish.
(3) Top with whipped cream.

☛INGREDIENTS:

4 cups of rhubarb, cut into bite-size pieces
2 cups of sugar
2 cups of water
juice and grated zest of 1 orange
2/3 cups of tapioca (not pearl type)

SERVES 8

STEAMED
CHOCOLATE PUDDING

(1) Sift together the flour, baking powder, and salt.
(2) Add the sugar, the egg, butter, chocolate, vanilla, and milk. Beat thoroughly.
(3) Pour batter into a well buttered mold with a tight-fitting lid.
(4) Place on a rack in a large pot filled with enough water to come halfway up mold. Steam for 2 hours.
(5) Remove from steamer and remove lid. Let the pudding sit for 20 minutes before unmolding.
(6) Serve warm or at room temperature with whipped cream, ice cream, and/or chocolate sauce.

NOTE: This pudding tastes better the second day.

☛INGREDIENTS:

1-1/2 cups of flour
1-1/2 tsp. of baking powder
1/4 tsp. of salt
1/2 cup of sugar
1 egg, well beaten
2 tbls. of butter, melted
1-1/2 squares of unsweetened chocolate, melted
1/2 tsp. of vanilla
1/2 cup of milk

SERVES 6

VANILLA EXTRACT

(1) Place vodka/rum in an wide-mouthed jar.
(2) Add the split vanilla beans.
(3) Store in your cupboard for 2 months.
(4) Remove vanilla. (See note)
(5) Use as you would store-bought vanilla.

NOTE: Use leftover vanilla beans to make vanilla sugar. Place vanilla beans in a jar containing 1 lb. of sugar. The sugar will take on the taste of the vanilla and is excellent when sprinkled on toast.

☛INGREDIENTS:

1 pt. of vodka or dark rum
2 vanilla beans, split

MAKES 1 PINT

LEMON EXTRACT

(1) Place vodka in an wide-mouthed jar.
(2) Add the lemon zest.
(3) Store in your cupboard for 2 months.
(4) Strain out the lemon zest and discard.
(5) Use as you would store-bought
    lemon extract.

☞INGREDIENTS:

1 pt. of vodka
zest from 4 lemons

MAKES 1 PINT

ORANGE EXTRACT

(1) Place vodka in an wide-mouthed jar.
(2) Add the orange zest.
(3) Store in your cupboard for 2 months.
(4) Strain out the orange zest and discard.
(5) Use as you would store-bought
    orange extract.

☞INGREDIENTS:

1 pt. of vodka
zest from 2 oranges

MAKES 1 PINT

LEMON CATSUP

(1) Grate the rind of the lemons.
(2) Sprinkle the salt over the lemon rind, mixed ground spices, sugar, horseradish, and shallot.
(3) Add the lemon juice and let stand for 3 hours in a cool place.
(4) Boil this mixture in a porcelain coated pot for 1/2 hour.
(5) Pour into a glass, china, or stone container.
(6) Let stand for a month, stirring well once a day.
(7) Strain and pour into hot sterilized jars.
(8) Seal, using the hot water bath method.

NOTE: This is a good seasoning for fish sauces and soups.

NOTE: To protect against spoilage, a hot water bath is recommended. This simple but important process is beyond the scope of this book. Refer to any full-sized cookbook, canning pamphlet, or cookbook on preserves for specific details.

☛INGREDIENTS:

12 large lemons, rind and juice
4 tbls. of ground white mustard seed
1 tbls. of ground turmeric
1 tbls. of ground white pepper
1 tsp. of ground cloves
1 tsp. of ground mace
1/4 tsp. of cayenne
2 tbls. of granulated sugar
2 tbls. of grated horseradish
1 shallot, finely minced
2 tbls. of salt

MAKES 1 PINT

MUSHROOM CATSUP

(1) Lay mushrooms and salt in alternate layers in an earthenware pot.
(2) Set aside for 6 hours.
(3) Break mushrooms into small pieces.
(4) Set mushrooms in a cool place for 3 days, stirring thoroughly every morning.
(5) Strain and measure out the juice, discarding the mushrooms.
(6) Add spices.
(7) Set in a stone jar and cover closely.
(8) Set jar in a pot of boiling water and boil hard for 5 hours.
(9) Remove from flame and place mixture into a porcelain coated pot.
(10) Gently boil for 30 minutes.
(11) Let this mixture stand overnight in a cool place until settled and clear.
(12) Carefully pour off liquid without disturbing the sediment.
(13) Pour into small hot sterilized jars and seal, using the hot water bath method.

☛INGREDIENTS:

2 lbs. of mushrooms
1/4 lb. of salt

To every qt. of juice allow:
1 tsp. of ground allspice
1 tsp. of ground ginger
1/2 tsp. of powdered mace
1 pinch of cayenne pepper

NOTE: To protect against spoilage, a hot water bath is recommended. This simple but important process is beyond the scope of this book. Refer to any full-sized cookbook, canning pamphlet, or cookbook on preserves for specific details.

OYSTER CATSUP

(1) Chop oysters and boil in their own liquor with the vinegar (skim off the scum as it appears) for 3 minutes.
(2) Strain through a colander lined with cheesecloth.
(3) Return liquid to clean pot and add sherry, salt, pepper, and mace.
(4) Boil for 15 minutes.
(5) Remove from flame and cool.
(6) Pour into hot sterilized jars and seal, using the hot water bath method.

NOTE: To protect against spoilage, a hot water bath is recommended. This simple but important process is beyond the scope of this book. Refer to any full-sized cookbook, canning pamphlet, or cookbook on preserves for specific details.

☛INGREDIENTS:

1 qt. of oysters
1/2 cup of cider vinegar
1/2 cup of sherry
1 tbls. of salt
1 pinch of cayenne pepper
1/4 tsp. of mace

TOMATO CATSUP
COOKED

(1) Boil tomato pulp, brown sugar, onions, garlic, and salt until thick.
(2) Put through a sieve and then return to stove.
(3) Add the remaining ingredients.
(4) Bring to a boil.
(5) Pour into hot sterilized jars.
(6) Seal, using the hot water bath method.

NOTE: To protect against spoilage, a hot water bath is recommended. This simple but important process is beyond the scope of this book. Refer to any full-sized cookbook, canning pamphlet, or cookbook on preserves for specific details.

☛ INGREDIENTS:

2 tbls. of salt
2 qts. of ripe tomato pulp
3 tbls. of brown sugar
2 onions, finely chopped
1 clove of garlic
2 tbls. of mustard
1 tsp. of cinnamon
1 tbls. of allspice
1/2 tsp. of cayenne pepper
1/2 tsp. of ground cloves
1/2 tsp. of nutmeg
1/2 cup of cider vinegar

MAKES 1 PINT

INDIAN CHUTNEY

(1) Pare, core, and chop the apples.
(2) Chop and add the peppers.
(3) Chop and add the onions.
(4) Add the raisins and vinegar.
(5) Put mixture into a large kettle and simmer for 2 hours.
(6) Add the sugar and seasonings and simmer for an additional hour.
(7) Pour into hot sterilized jars.
(8) Seal, using the hot water bath method.
(9) Wait at least 10 days before serving.
(10) Serve with lamb.

NOTE: To protect against spoilage, a hot water bath is recommended. This simple but important process is beyond the scope of this book. Refer to any full-sized cookbook, canning pamphlet, or cookbook on preserves for specific details.

☛INGREDIENTS:

15 sour apples
2 green peppers
2 large onions
1 cup of raisins
1 qt. of cider vinegar
2 cups of brown sugar
2 tbls. of white mustard seeds
2 tbls. of ground ginger
2 tbls. of salt

MAKES 5 PINTS

MINT CHUTNEY

(1) Chop the tomatoes.

(2) Add the salt and mix.

(3) Let stand overnight.

(4) In the morning, drain and then soak the tomatoes in cold water for 3 minutes.

(5) Drain the tomatoes again.

(6) Chop and add the apples, onions, raisins, peppers and the mint.

(7) Heat the vinegar.

(8) Add sugar and mustard to the vinegar.

(9) Mix all of the ingredients together and simmer for 30 minutes.

(10) Pour into hot sterilized jars.

(11) Seal, using the hot water bath method.

(12 Wait at least 10 days before serving.

(13) Serve with lamb.

NOTE: To protect against spoilage, a hot water bath is recommended. This simple but important process is beyond the scope of this book. Refer to any full-sized cookbook, canning pamphlet, or cookbook on preserves for specific details.

☞INGREDIENTS:

1/2 lb. of ripe tomatoes

2 tsp. of salt

1 lb. of tart apples

12 small onions

3 large peppers

1-1/3 cup of raisins

1/2 cup of chopped mint leaves

3 cups of cider vinegar

2 cups of granulated sugar

2 tsp. of dry mustard

PEACH CHUTNEY

(1) Peel the fresh peaches and chop into small pieces.
(2) Boil the peaches in one pint of vinegar until tender (approx. 1/2 hour).
(3) Finely chop the onion and ginger.
(4) Make a syrup of the sugar and remaining vinegar.
(5) Add all of the ingredients to this syrup and cook for 1 hour or until thick, stirring frequently.
(6) Pour into hot sterilized jars and seal, using hot water bath.

NOTE: To protect against spoilage, a hot water bath is recommended. This simple but important process is beyond the scope of this book. Refer to any full-sized cookbook, canning pamphlet, or cookbook on preserves for specific details.

☛INGREDIENTS:

6 lbs. of fresh peaches
2 pts. of white vinegar
2 small onions
1/2 lb. of fresh ginger
1-1/4 lbs. of brown sugar
1-2 tbls. of red chili powder
1/4 cup of mustard seed
1/2 lb. of raisins
1/3 cup of salt

MAKES 5-1/2 PINTS

LEMON VINEGAR

(1) Pour cider vinegar into a
     wide-mouthed jar.
(2) Cut rind off each lemon.
(3) Stud lemon rind with whole cloves.
(4) Close jar tightly.
(5) Store for 2 weeks in a cool, dark cupboard.
(6) Remove and discard lemon
     rind and cloves.

☛INGREDIENTS:

2 cups of apple cider vinegar
rind of 3 lemons
30 whole cloves

MAKES 1 PINT

RASPBERRY VINEGAR

(1) Heat vinegar until very hot.
(2) Place berries in a jar.
(3) Pour hot vinegar over berries.
(4) Cover and let stand 3-5 days.
(5) Strain vinegar through a jelly bag or colander lined with cheese cloth.
(6) Discard berries.
(7) Add sugar.
(8) Store vinegar in a cool, dark, cupboard to preserve the color.

NOTE: Do not store in a jar with a metal top as the vinegar will erode the metal. Use wet brown paper tied down with twine, cork, or glass stoppers.

NOTE: When roasting duck, baste with this vinegar.

Strawberry Vinegar
Substitute 1 pt. of fresh strawberries instead of raspberries.

☛INGREDIENTS:

1 qt. of white vinegar
1 pt. of fresh raspberries
3 tbls. of sugar

MAKES 1 QUART

BREAD AND BUTTER PICKLES

(1) Sprinkle salt over cucumbers and onions.
(2) Store from 3 hours to overnight. Toss once during this time.
(3) Drain and rinse with cold water.
(4) In a saucepan, mix together the vinegar, sugar, mustard seed, turmeric, and celery seed.
(5) Bring to a simmer over a medium flame.
(6) Add the cucumbers and onions and bring back to a simmer.
(7) Simmer for 2-3 minutes. Stir with a large spoon to circulate the cucumbers.
(8) Pour into hot sterilized jars and seal, using the hot water bath method.

NOTE: Unsealed jars will keep in your refrigerator for up to 4 weeks.

NOTE: To protect against spoilage, a hot water bath is recommended. This simple but important process is beyond the scope of this book. Refer to any full-sized cookbook, canning pamphlet, or cookbook on preserves for specific details.

☞ INGREDIENTS:

25 - 30 kirby cucumbers, sliced
8 onions, sliced
1/2 cup of pickling salt
5 cups of white vinegar
6 cups of sugar
2 tbls. of mustard seed
1 tbls. of turmeric
1 tbls. of celery seed

PICCALILLI

(1) In a large pot mix tomatoes, cabbage, onions, and peppers.
(2) Sprinkle salt over the vegetables.
(3) Let this mixture stand overnight.
(4) Drain and rinse with cold water.
(5) In a saucepan, mix together the sugar and spices.
(6) Add the vegetables and enough vinegar to cover.
(7) Bring to a hard boil.
(8) Reduce the heat and simmer for 20 minutes.
(9) Place in hot sterilized jars and seal, using the hot water bath method.

NOTE: This is a good substitute for pickle relish.

NOTE: To protect against spoilage, a hot water bath is recommended. This simple but important process is beyond the scope of this book. Refer to any full-sized cookbook, canning pamphlet, or cookbook on preserves for specific details.

☛INGREDIENTS:

16 green tomatoes, chopped
1 small cabbage, chopped
8 onions, chopped
5 green peppers, chopped
2 sweet red peppers, chopped
2 tbls. of pickling salt
4 cups of sugar
grated horseradish to taste
2 tsp. of celery seed
1 tbls. of mustard seed
1 tbls. of dry mustard
1-1/2 tsp. of ground ginger
1/4 tsp. ground cinnamon
1/4 tsp. of whole cloves
2/4 tsp. of mace
white vinegar to cover

MAKES 4 PINTS

PICKLE RELISH

(1) Grind up tomatoes, onions, cabbage, and peppers using a meat grinder.
(2) Sprinkle salt over this mixture.
(3) Store overnight. Toss once during this time.
(4) Drain and rinse with cold water.
(5) In a saucepan, mix together the vinegar, water, sugar, mustard seed, turmeric, and celery seed.
(6) Bring to a simmer over a medium flame.
(7) Add the vegetables and bring back to a simmer.
(8) Simmer for 2-3 minutes. Stir with a large spoon to circulate the vegetables.
(9) Place in hot sterilized jars and seal, using the hot water bath method.

NOTE: Unsealed jars will keep in your refrigerator for up to 4 weeks.

NOTE: To protect against spoilage, a hot water bath is recommended. This simple but important process is beyond the scope of this book. Refer to any full-sized cookbook, canning pamphlet, or cookbook on preserves for specific details.

☛INGREDIENTS:

10 green tomatoes
4 cups of onions
4 cups of cabbage
12 green peppers, seeded and de-ribbed
6 red peppers, seeded and de-ribbed
1/3 cup of pickling salt
4 cups of white vinegar
2 cups of water
6 cups of sugar
2 tbls. of mustard seed
1-1/2 tsp. of turmeric
1 tbls. of celery seed

MAKES 6 PINTS

THREE-DAY DILL PICKLES

(1) Heat enough pickling brine to cover cucumbers.
(2) In a large wide-mouthed jar, layer cucumbers, garlic, and dill.
(3) Pour hot vinegar mixture over cucumber layers.
(4) Top with rye bread.
(5) Store at room temperature for 3-4 days.
(6) Refrigerate.

NOTE: If you prefer, process using the hot water bath method. A hot water bath will protect against spoilage. This simple but important process is beyond the scope of this book. Refer to any full-sized cookbook, canning pamphlet, or cookbook on preserves for specific details.

☛INGREDIENTS:

Pickling Brine
1 part vinegar to 2 parts water
  with 1/2 cup of
          pickling salt

1 peck of kirby cucumbers
6 garlic cloves, minced
2 bunches of dill
3 slices of rye bread

MAKES 4 QUARTS

WATERMELON PICKLE

(1) Remove skin and pink meat of watermelon from the rind.
(2) Cut rind into 2-inch cubes.
(3) Place in a bowl with enough pickling brine to cover and store overnight.
(4) In the morning, drain and rinse the rind.
(5) Place rind in a pot, cover with cold water and cook until just tender.
(6) Place cinnamon and cloves in cheesecloth and wrap up into a bag.
(7) In a saucepan, mix together the vinegar, 1 cup of water, sugar, and the spice bag.
(8) Bring to a simmer for 15 minutes.
(9) Remove spice bag and add the watermelon rind and lemon; bring back to a simmer, until the rind is clear.
(10) Place in hot sterilized jars and seal using the hot water bath method.

NOTE: To protect against spoilage, a hot water bath is recommended. This simple but important process is beyond the scope of this book. Re-fer to any full-sized cookbook, canning pamphlet, or cookbook on preserves for specific details.

☛INGREDIENTS:

Pickling Brine
1/4 cup of pickling salt for each
 qt. of water

1 large watermelon
1 cup of white vinegar
1 cup of water
2 cups of sugar
2 tbls. of mustard seed
1 tbls. of broken cinnamon
 stick (3 pieces)
1-1/2 tsp. of whole cloves
1 small piece of cheesecloth
1/2 lemon, thinly sliced

MAKES 6 PINTS

BEACH PLUM JELLY

(1) Fill a large pot 1/2 - 3/4 full with beach plums.
(2) Add water.
(3) Simmer slowly for 30 minutes.
(4) Put this fruit mixture through a food mill to remove skins and seeds.
(5) Pour the remaining mixture into a jelly bag.
(6) Hang the jelly bag over a bowl until all of the juice has dripped out.
(7) Leave the juice in the bowl and let sit in the open for 12 hours.
(8) Cover the bowl and place it in the refrigerator for 24 hours (this causes all the natural sugars to settle to the bottom; you will not use these sugars).
(9) Pour juice out, being sure not to disturb the sediment on the bottom.
(10) Measure juice and add correct amount of sugar.
(11) Boil to soft jelly stage; it will sheet off the spoon.
(12) Pour into hot sterilized jars and seal with paraffin wax.

☛INGREDIENTS:

beach plums
1 cup of water
1 cup of sugar to each cup of fruit juice

NOTE: Beach Plums can be found growing on the dunes at the beach.

NOTE: To protect against spoilage, I recommend you seal each jar with paraffin wax. This simple but important process is beyond the scope of this book. Refer to any full-sized cookbook, canning pamphlet, or cookbook on preserves for specific details.

GRAPE JELLY

(1) Fill a large pot 1/2 - 3/4 full with grapes.
(2) Add water.
(3) Simmer slowly for 30 minutes.
(4) Put this fruit mixture through a food mill to remove skins and seeds.
(5) Pour the remaining mixture into a jelly bag.
(6) Hang the jelly bag over a bowl until all of the juice has dripped out.
(7) Leave the juice in the bowl and let sit in the open for 12 hours.
(8) Cover the bowl and place in the refrigerator for 24 hours (this causes all the natural sugars to settle to the bottom; you will not use these sugars).
(9) Pour juice out, being sure not to disturb the sediment on the bottom.
(10) Measure juice and add correct amount of sugar.
(11) Boil to soft jelly stage; it will sheet off the spoon.
(12) Pour into hot sterilized jars and top with paraffin wax.

☛INGREDIENTS:

Concord grapes
1 cup of water
1 cup of sugar to each cup of fruit juice

NOTE: To protect against spoilage, I recommend you seal each jar with paraffin wax. This simple but important process is beyond the scope of this book. Refer to any full-sized cookbook, canning pamphlet, or cookbook on preserves for specific details.

STRAWBERRY JAM

(1) Boil the currant juice with strawberries for 1/2 hour, stirring constantly.
(2) Add the sugar and boil rapidly for approximately 20 minutes, occasionally skimming off foam carefully.
(3) Pour into small hot sterilized jars and top with paraffin wax.

NOTE: To protect against spoilage, I recommend you seal each jar with paraffin wax. This simple but important process is beyond the scope of this book. Refer to any full-sized cookbook, canning pamphlet, or cookbook on preserves for specific details.

☞INGREDIENTS:

4 lbs. of strawberries, hulled
3 lbs. of sugar
1 pt. of currant juice

MAKES 8 PINTS

BRANDIED CHERRIES

(1) In a saucepan, mix the sugar and water.
(2) Bring to a boil, stirring constantly.
(3) Remove syrup from flame and cool until warm.
(4) Pour over the cherries.
(5) Let them stand for 1 hour.
(6) Put all into a large pot and bring to a boil slowly.
(7) Boil for 5 minutes, then remove fruit.
(8) Boil the syrup for another 20 minutes.
(9) Remove from the flame and add the brandy, immediately.
(10) Divide the fruit equally into hot sterilized jars and fill with hot syrup.
(11) Seal using the hot water bath method.

NOTE: You can also substitute berries in this recipe, such as strawberries, raspberries, blackberries, etc.

NOTE: To protect against spoilage, a hot water bath is recommended. This simple but important process is beyond the scope of this book. Refer to any full-sized cookbook, canning pamphlet, or cookbook on preserves for specific details.

☛INGREDIENTS:

2-1/2 lbs. of sugar
5 oz. of water
5 lbs. of cherries
1 pt. of best white brandy

MAKES 6 PINTS

BRANDIED PEACHES

(1) Peel peaches by dipping them in boiling and then cold water.
(2) In a saucepan, mix the sugar and water.
(3) Bring to a boil.
(4) Add the fruit and boil for 5 minutes.
(5) Gently remove the fruit.
(6) Boil the syrup for another 15 minutes or until it has thickened.
(7) Remove the pot from flame and immediately add the brandy.
(8) Pour off red liquor from the peaches, if any has formed.
(9) Seal using the hot water bath method.
(10) Divide the fruit equally into hot sterilized jars and fill with hot syrup.

☞INGREDIENTS:

4 lbs. of peaches
4 lbs. of sugar
2 cups of water
1 pt. of best white brandy

MAKES 6 PINTS

NOTE: The leftover syrup can be used as a delicious glaze for Cornish game hens or as flavoring in a peach frosty.

NOTE: To protect against spoilage, a hot water bath is recommended. This simple but important process is beyond the scope of this book. Refer to any full-sized cookbook, canning pamphlet, or cookbook on preserves for specific details.

BRANDIED PEARS

(1) Peel pears by dipping them in boiling water then cold water.
(2) In a saucepan, mix the sugar and water.
(3) Bring to a boil.
(4) Add the fruit and boil for 5 minutes.
(5) Remove the fruit gently.
(6) Boil the syrup for another 15 minutes or until it has thickened.
(7) Remove the pot from the flame and immediately add the brandy.
(8) Pour off liquor from the pears, if any has formed.
(9) Divide the fruit equally into hot sterilized jars and fill with hot syrup.
(10) Place in hot sterilized jars and seal, using the hot water bath method.

NOTE: To protect against spoilage, a hot water bath is recommended. This simple but important process is beyond the scope of this book. Refer to any full-sized cookbook, canning pamphlet or cookbook on preserves for specific details.

☛INGREDIENTS:

4 lbs. of pears, pealed
4 lbs. of sugar
2 cups water
1 pt. of best white brandy

MAKES 6 PINTS

CORN PRESERVE

(1) Mix all of the ingredients in a saucepan.
(2) Cover with water and bring to a boil.
(3) Pour the corn mixture into pint-sized sterilized jars.
(4) Seal, using hot water bath method.

NOTE: To protect against spoilage, a hot water bath is recommended. This simple but important process is beyond the scope of this book. Refer to any full-sized cookbook, canning pamphlet or cookbook on preserves for specific details.

☛INGREDIENTS:

9 cups of corn
1 cup of sugar
3/4 cup of salt

MAKES 4-5 PINTS

GREEN BEAN PRESERVE

(1) Cook beans in boiling water for 3 minutes.
(2) Measure out 6 quarts.
(3) Mix all the ingredients.
(4) Fill hot sterilized jars with mixture.
(5) Seal, using hot water bath method.

NOTE: To protect against spoilage, a hot water bath is recommended. This simple but important process is beyond the scope of this book. Refer to any full-sized cookbook, canning pamphlet or cookbook on preserves for specific details.

☛INGREDIENTS:

6 qts. of green beans, cooked
3 tbls. of sugar
3/4 cup of white vinegar
3 tbls. of salt

MAKES 12 PINTS

RIPE TOMATO PRESERVES

(1) Mix the tomatoes and sugar.
(2) Let sit overnight.
(3) Drain off the syrup and boil it; be sure to skim off all of the foam.
(4) Add the tomatoes and boil gently for 20 minutes.
(5) Remove the tomatoes with a perforated spoon.
(6) Boil the syrup down until it thickens.
(7) Add the lemon juice just before you remove the syrup from the flame.
(8) Divide the fruit equally into hot sterilized jars and fill with hot syrup.
(9) When cold, seal with paraffin wax.

NOTE: To protect against spoilage, I recommend you seal each jar with paraffin wax. This simple but important process is beyond the scope of this book. Refer to any full-sized cookbook, canning pamphlet or cookbook on preserves for specific details.

☛INGREDIENTS:

7 lbs. of round yellow, or egg tomatoes, peeled and cubed
3-1/2 lbs. of sugar
juice of 3 lemons

MAKES APPROXIMATELY
14 PINTS

BEEF TEA

(1) Place meat and salt in jar and cover tightly.
(2) Simmer in a pot filled with water for
    3-4 hours.
(3) Remove and discard meat.
(4) Serve hot in small teacups.

NOTE: Beef tea was used for medicinal
purposes.

☛INGREDIENTS:

1 lbs. of top round, cubed
a pinch of salt
1 qt. glass jar with lid

SERVES 4

HOT APPLE CIDER

(1) Place the spices in the cheesecloth and tie up into a small bag.
(2) Pour apple cider into a saucepan.
(3) Add cider and simmer for 15 minutes.
(4) Remove spice bag.
(5) Serve immediately.

☛INGREDIENTS:

1 qt. of apple cider
1 stick of cinnamon
4 whole cloves
4 whole allspice
1 small piece of cheesecloth

SERVES 4

HOT COCOA

(1) In a sauce pan, mix together cocoa, sugar, and salt.
(2) Slowly add the water.
(3) Boil gently for 2 minutes, stirring until slightly thickened.
(4) Reduce the flame and add the milk.
(5) Heat slowly until scalding hot.
(6) Add vanilla extract.
(7) Serve immediately, topped with whipped cream.

☛INGREDIENTS:

6 tbls. of unsweetened cocoa
6 tbls. of granulated sugar
1/4 tsp. of salt
1 cup of water
3 cups of milk
1/2 tsp. of vanilla extract

SERVES 6

CURRANT PUNCH

(1) Whip the currant jelly to a froth.
(2) Add to boiling water to dissolve.
(3) Add the sugar and stir to dissolve sugar.
(4) Add the orange and lemon juice.
(5) Cool and serve diluted with mineral water or ice water.
(6) Garnish with orange slices.

☛INGREDIENTS:

2 cups of currant jelly
1 pt. of boiling water
1/4 cup of sugar
3 oranges
2 lemons
mineral water
halved orange slices

SERVES 8

DIXIE PUNCH

(1) Squeeze the juice from the lemons and oranges.
(2) Crush strawberries.
(3) In a saucepan, mix sugar and the water.
(4) Heat until all of the sugar is dissolved, stirring constantly.
(5) Add the lemon juice, orange juice, and strawberries to the sugar syrup.
(6) Serve over ice.

☛INGREDIENTS:

6 lemons
4 oranges
1 pt. of fresh strawberries
1 gal. of water
2 cups of sugar

MAKES 1-1/4 GALLONS

GINGERADE

(1) In a saucepan, mix sugar and sugar and boil for 20 minutes then set aside until cool.
(2) Cut the ginger root and lemons into thin slices.
(3) Add to 1 qt. of boiling water and boil for 15 minutes.
(4) Cool and then strain, discarding the ginger root and lemon.
(5) When cool add the fruit juice and sugar syrup to taste.
(6) Serve over cracked ice.

☛INGREDIENTS:

1 cup of sugar
2 cups of water
2 oz. of fresh ginger root, peeled
2 lemons
1 qt. of boiling water
1 cup of orange, pineapple, or other fruit juice
Ice water or cracked ice

SERVES 4

GRAPE JUICE

(1) Crush grapes and boil, in the water,
    for 15 minutes.
(2) Process through a food mill.
(3) Add sugar and heat until dissolved.
(4) Strain through a jelly bag.
(5) Heat until the juice reaches
    boiling point.
(6) Pour into hot sterilized jars.
(7) Seal, using hot water bath.

☛INGREDIENTS:

12 lbs. of grapes
3 qts. of water
3 lbs. of sugar

MAKES 2 GALLONS

GRAPE FRAPPE

(1) Boil water and sugar for 20 minutes.
(2) Add fruit juices.
(3) Dilute with water and serve over ice.

Grape Frappe Soda
(1) Make the juice as described in the
    above recipe.
(2) Dilute juice with seltzer.
(3) Serve over ice.

☛INGREDIENTS:

7 cups of water
3-1/2 cups of sugar
5-1/2 cups of grape juice
1/2 cup of lemon juice
1 cup of orange juice
cracked ice

MAKES 1/2 GALLON

INDEX

Traditional Country Life Recipe Books from
Brick Tower Press
Apple Companion
Chocolate Companion

Forthcoming Titles
Herb Companion
Clambake
Thanksgiving Cookery
Victorian Christmas Cookbook

Mail Order and General Information

Many of our titles are carried by your local book store or gift and museum shop. If they do not already carry our line please ask them to write us for information.

If you are unable to purchase our titles from your local shop we made them available through mail order. Just send us a check or money order for $9.95 per title with $1.00 postage to the address below or call us Monday through Friday, 9 AM to 5PM, EST.

Send all mail order, book club, and special sales requests to the address below or call us. We would like to hear from you.

Brick Tower Press
1230 Park Avenue, 10th Floor
New York, NY 10128

Telephone & Facsimile
1-212-427-7139
1-800-68-BRICK

America OnLine: McKee